FASCINATION OF
ROME

SPLENDID IMAGES
RECOUNT
THE ETERNAL CITY

Editor:

LOZZI ROMA s.a.s.

Via Filippo Nicolai, 91 - 00136 Roma

Tel. (+39) 06 35497051 - 06 97841668

Fax (+39) 06 35497074

E-mail: info@lozziroma.com

Web: www.gruppolozzi.it

Printed by:

CSC Grafica s.r.l.- Guidonia (Roma)

E-mail: info@cscgrafica.it - Web: www.cscgrafica.it

Photographs:

Lozzi Roma s.a.s.

Millenium s.r.l.

Archivio Fotografico della Fabbrica di San Pietro

Archivio Fotografico Musei e Gallerie Pontificie

Scala Archives - Firenze

Made in Italy

FASCINATION OF ROME

Every city has its own fragrance, its color, something different from any other that makes it live in the memory - or in the dreams - of those who are far away; a unique charm that expresses and condenses its intimate nature. And just as no two cities in the world are alike, so their perfumes, nostalgia and emotions, the sounds by which they speak to us, are infinitely varied.

There is a poem, a symphony of each city; and if Gershwin set to music the rhythm of New York and the verve of Paris, no one else like Respighi turned the essence of Rome into unmistakable sound; so that just listening to his melody is to catch something of the city's charm.

Rome is now a great attraction for world tourism; her appeal still as strong as when Goethe, Mendelssohn, Shelley, Browning, Wagner, Ruskin and Chateaubriand, to mention only a few of the greatest, experienced it in their day. Yet she is certainly not a star among the cities of today, like Paris or New York; she lacks their glamour and prestige, their spaciousness and magnificent perspectives, the vast range of activities, the zest, the vitality, their intense poetry...

She is not a city in the modern sense of the word, and less than all a cosmopolitan metropolis: what then, is the secret of her constant charm and unfailing power? No doubt it is partly due to her museums, among the richest in the world; but cities do not live by museums alone: there is their atmosphere, the people, the life that flows there...

It is perhaps her measure - the size of a city that neither startles nor oppresses, being big but not huge. A place to be enjoyed and not endured, where everything is more accessible and from which man does not feel excluded.

Hers is a distant, lazy charm, for the way time slowly glides by, so that her beauties may be enjoyed at leisure, a perpetual reminder of the past, made of ancient stones and profound silences that everyday stupidity tries in vain to penetrate with the futile noises of the usual traffic. The legendary charm of a city where, in spite of everything, one can still follow the favorite routes of Stendhal or, like the romantic Keats, retreat in such ideal secluded places as the Palatine, among great ruins which saw the golden age pass by, and now look down indifferently at the cars wheeling around them, as a proud colossus might watch a swarm of ludicrous insects.

All styles, periods and great movements in art are represented in this city, which takes three days to tour and three years, at least, to get to know. It is equally invaluable, however, to live in its atmosphere, to enjoy the air of Rome, her mild climate and cloudy skies over the wide incomparable views of her churches and roofs; the afternoons along the Tiber, sunsets from the Pincio, and the soft Roman nights...

It is like the warm bliss of a lizard basking in the sun, and one never tires of it; it is a life full of contrasts: one feels alone, and at the same time in company, as there is freedom here without desert, and height without mountains.

Rome is still largely an individualistic city, where a keen mind cannot feel itself as part of a mass, or a cipher, but simply human. There is the pleasure, rare today, of giving one's imagination rein – and the leisure to enjoy it, if one dares.

So many men, so many suits – and each suit is a different character! One can stroll for hours without being bored, and with no haste of course, as time is nothing here, obliterated by three thousand years.

The best way to see Rome is on foot. Besides, there is no other choice, in a Capital with no large subway nor avenues, where the car is a fever clouding more brains every day. Nor can you stay indoors – while Rome invites you out into beautiful squares or sumptuous courtyards, to hear clear water constantly spring out from the coolness of ornate fountains and mossy niches; to enjoy her gardens on a sunny day, or the changing tints of her many palaces, turning from ochres and pinks to old golds and yellows as the hours go by, and fading towards evening into the reds of a flaming sunset.

Go through the center of Rome, in the quiet hours of an early afternoon, and you will shortly relive dreams you had long fancied under a paler sky. Certainly, not everyone can enjoy it this way, but the tourist can; he is absolute master of himself, free of bonds and limits, duties or schedules, and similar calamities; open to the indefinable joy of feeling really alive, lighthearted, and rich, since his time belongs entirely to him, like a fortune to be squandered as he pleases.

Like all the travelers of the past, he will feel this city is his – as Byron wrote in his poem: "Oh Rome, my country, city of the soul!".

And he will see, through eyes dimmed by emotion, an ancient city of domes and rare obelisks, superb statues, precious fountains and imposing ruins of changeable colors, where sacred and profane confront each other in a multitude of petrified saints and naked pagan figures, trophies and crosses, Popes and beautiful goddesses...

In the daily contrast of flesh and spirit, between sense and belief – here more obvious, each day, than elsewhere in the world – still lies in fact part of the charm of Rome, this odd city that holds the greatest traces of its immense empire, while it encloses, within itself, a foreign state peaceful and sovereign, the smallest state with the biggest dome on earth.

ROME THROUGH THE CENTURIES

ANCIENT ROME

Tradition has it that Rome was founded by Romulus, the first king, in 753 BC. More than a millennium passed from its birth to its decline, which followed the first waves of barbarian invasion.

What can still be admired today in almost every corner of the city center are mainly ruins dating from the Republican age, which began with the expulsion of the last King, Tarquin the Proud (509 BC) and especially the remains of the subsequent Imperial age, which lasted from the rule of Augustus (27 AD) to that of Romulus Augustulus (476).

The changes Rome has undergone through its history of over 2750 years have not effaced the traces left by time, untidily superimposed perhaps, but which ultimately form a harmonious palimpsest. While temples of the Republican period may be seen in the sacred area of Largo di Torre Argentina or near the Foro Boario, Imperial Rome reveals itself in its full splendor in the area of the Roman Forum, the Palatine and the imperial Forums, with the incomparable outline of the Coliseum in the background. It was in fact at the beginning of the imperial times that one of the most exciting periods of Roman culture began, vividly expressed in the works of Virgil, Horace, Ovid and Titus Livy. In the arts and urban development, this was the age in which the empire began to celebrate its own glory. Triumphal arches, extraordinary monuments and ever more astounding imperial forums were built to exalt the greatness of Rome and its emperors, whose deification after their death was celebrated by the erection of grandiose mausoleums.

Rome, *Caput mundi*, a metropolis with already more than a million inhabitants at the end of the second century, reached the peak of its splendor with the Flavians, when the Coliseum, the Baths of Titus, Domitian s Palace and Stadium (present-day Piazza Navona) were built, as were other buildings which still inspire wonder in those who see them today.

CHRISTIAN ROME

It was a Roman emperor, Constantine (fourth century) who initiated the building of the first great Christian basilicas such as St John the Lateran, St Lawrence outside the Walls and above all St Peter s in the Vatican.

In the following century, the Church began to gain enough strength and autonomy to begin the construction of basilicas which are now well-known places of worship. The basilicas of St Mary Major and St Paul date from this period. The Rome of the popes also grew by adapting and transforming the pre-existing buildings to the needs of worship, using the enormous quantity of marble, metal and other materials these monuments provided. The celebration of the Church s spiritual and temporal primacy paved the way to the urban rebirth of Rome which began in the Middle Ages and was fully established by the beginning of the 15th century.

From that time, all the pontiffs, such as Nicholas V, who planned the demolition of the Constantinian Basilica of St Peter in order to build the new one, or Julius II, who commissioned works by Michelangelo and Rafael, strove to increase the magnificence of their pontificates.

The transformation which sprang from the council of Trent in the 16th century, following the Protestant Reformation, produced a new impetus focused on strengthening the Roman church also through art. Churches, squares, fountains, built by artists like Bernini, became instruments for the renewal of Rome s image and the prevention of the spread of the Protestant doctrines. Even now that the temporal power of the Papal State has ended (since 1870) and the pontiffs have withdrawn to Vatican City, the Church s role and presence in the city of Rome are far from having disappeared. The Jubilee of the Year 2000 involved the entire social and urban fabric of the city, once again asserting this evident indissoluble interrelationship.

FROM RENAISSANCE ROME TO THE 19TH CENTURY

The continuation of the Church s great influence in the European courts gave rise to a flourishing urban rebirth from the second half of the 15th century. In this time important construction projects were accomplished for the nobility, such as the building of a palace for Cardinal Farnese (the future Pope Paul III) in 1516, the reorganization of the Capitol, entrusted to Michelangelo by Paul III in 1536, the construction of villas with gardens, squares, such as Campo de Fiori and Piazza Farnese, streets such as Via Giulia and a new network of roads conceived by Pope Sixtus V for the hilly areas abandoned since the fall of the Roman Empire.

Renaissance architectural plans were modeled on examples of classical art, based on strict geometrical proportions. In the course of the 17th century, however, there was a break with the rigid rules of the Renaissance. While the grandiose settings of Baroque Rome were still modeled on the classical forms, they were given a dynamic interpretation, leaving room for creativity and an abundance of decorative elements. Bernini and Borromini, both Baroque architects, gave new shapes to fountains, façades, churches and squares, as can be seen in the spectacular Piazza Navona. The 18th century, on the other hand, was marked by the building of works with a great urban impact, of which the Trevi Fountain (1732) and the Spanish Steps (1735) are outstanding examples. From the Baroque, the fashion in the early 19th century reverted to the more simple Neoclassical structures, in the wake of the rediscovery of classical antiquity in all its forms.

The Neoclassical style, despite the fact that during the Napoleonic occupation there were phases when it was associated with imperial rhetoric, produced some works of great importance. Good examples are: Canova s sculptures, the beginning of systematic archeological excavation and Valadier s urban planning, including the remodeling of the Piazza del Popolo and the Pincio gardens.

MODERN ROME

The proclamation, in 1870, of Rome as the capital of the Kingdom of Italy led to radical changes. The transfer to the city of the royal court, the parliament and the ministries, gave rise to an immediate increase in the population and upset the tranquil atmosphere of papal Rome.

Under the impetus of the Risorgimento, ambitious projects were planned for the Kingdom s capital, but bureaucratic difficulties and the ensuing waves of speculation prevented the application of any kind of overall planning. Between the end of the 19th century and the first decades of the 20th, works such as the Victor Emanuel II monument were inaugurated, to whose grandiose proportions irreplaceable historical and artistic monuments were sacrificed: the new Montecitorio Palace, whose 17th century facade by Bernini, however, was saved, as were the Piazza della Repubblica and important streets such as Via XX Settembre.

The prevalent style in this period was Neo-Renaissance, flanked by Art Nouveau and perennial Neoclassicism. Whole neighborhoods were built, such as the Ludovisi district, with the famous Via Veneto, on the site of the splendid villa which bore that name. Later the imperial aspirations of the Fascist regime (1922/43) produced architectural works inspired by ancient Rome. In this period, further demolition of old mediaeval and Renaissance neighborhoods was carried out to make room for roads such as the Via dei Fori Imperiali, and the Via della Conciliazione. At the same time, plans for the expansion of the urban fabric toward the sea were established; in this context the EUR quarter was built.

Today the disorganized growth of the 50s and 60s seems to have come to an end; the city has returned to being the subject of fresh attention. Important projects are under way or are about to be developed for the enhancement and preservation of the artistic, archeological and human heritage, while the implementation of structural interventions compatible with the three millenniums of its history remain problematic.

22

48

59

60

74

THE IMAGES

1 - A marvelous sunset over St. Peter's Square Peter's Square. Very few states in the world can boast a vestibule like that created by St. Peter's Square; this extraordinary entrance gives the visitor a sense of serene and deep equilibrium.

2 - The Via Sacra. Shining columns reach upwards near the Arch of Titus, and old stones worn smooth by time and blocks of the ancient Appian way, where legions and chariot wheels passed from the various provinces of the Empire, still tell long stories and legends of buried times.

3 - The Roman Forum. White ruins of temples and of marble palaces, in the sumptuous disorder of the Roman Forum, remind us of the splendour which for ten centuries was at the center of a city that often dictated the destiny of the world.

4 - The Roman Forum. The center of civic and economic life in Republican times, the Forum maintained an important role also in the Imperial period. The Forum was crossed by the Via Sacra, which led to the Capitol Hill and also served as the route of the triumphal processions of the victorious generals.

5 - The Roman Forum. The Temple of Saturn (on the left) was erected by the Consul Titus Larcius (498 B.C.) It was always used as the public treasury, and as a repository for the standards of the Legions and the decrees of the Senate. On the right three columns remain of the Temple of Vespasian which was built by the son of Domitian in 94 A.D. and later restored by Septimius Severus.

6 - The Arch of Constantine was built by the Senate and the Roman people at the edge of the Forum, on the Via Sacra, in memory of the victory over Maxentius at Ponte Milvio in 312. It was built largely from pieces from the arches of Trajan and Marcus Aurelius.

7, 8, 9, 10, 11, 12 - The Colosseum. This immense amphitheater, whose imposing remains still allow us to admire its ancient splendor, was begun by Vespasian in 72 A.D. and completed by his son Titus in 80 A.D. It was built by Jewish prisoners. Its true name is the "Flavian Amphitheater", though it was commonly called the Colosseum, both for its proportions and its vicinity to the Colossus of Nero. The Colosseum had the same function as a modern giant

stadium, but the favorite spectacles in Roman times were the games of the Circus (*ludi circenses*), which probably had been invented in the late Republican era, with the intention of cultivating the war-like spirit that had made Romans the conquerors of the world. This was the origin of the professional gladiators,

who were trained to fight to the death, while wild beasts of every sort increased the horror of the show. Dion Cassius said that 9000 wild animals were killed in the one hundred days of celebrations which inaugurated the amphitheater. After the animals were killed and removed, the arena was often filled with water in order to stage naval battles. The Colosseum is elliptical in shape, 187 meters at its longest end and 155 meters at its shortest. The height of the exter-

nal ring reaches 50 meters from ground level. It was designed to accommodate an estimated 60,000 spectators. Around the exterior run three orders of arches, respectively adorned with Doric, Ionian and Corinthian columns, and a fourth floor with Corinthian pilasters. Of the 80 arches that make up the elliptical ring, four correspond to the entrances at the four axes, of which only the entrance of honor reserved for the Emperor remains. In the center of the

podium, called the suggestum, was the Emperor's seat; the rest of the podium was occupied by senators and members of the court. Then came the sections for the knights and civil and military tribunes. There were special places for married couples, for young men accompanied by their tutors, for families and servants, for women, and for servants. The Colosseum

was usually uncovered, but in case of rain it was covered by an immense velarium, which was maneuvered by two squads of sailors belonging to the fleets of Ravenna and Cape Misenum. These two squads also took part in the naval battles which were often staged in the amphitheater. When this amphitheater was in its full glory, it must have been a stupendous site of Roman greatness. But even today, after so many centuries, the Colosseum is the pride of Rome and a marvel to its visitors.

13 - Trajan's Markets located between Trajan's Forum and the lower slopes of the Quirinal, are magnificently preserved. They consist of a semicircular block of three stories and an upper level which includes a grandiose vaulted hall, in the form of a basilica.

14, 15, 16 - The Pantheon - the glory of Rome - is the city's only architecturally intact monument from classical times. Because of the inscription on the cornice of the portico, "M. Agrippa L.F. Cons. tertium fecit", for a long time it was believed that the Pantheon, as it stands today, had been built by Agrippa in 27 B.C. and dedicated to the gods of the Julian family; his temple was actually destroyed by a fire in 80 A.D., and completely redesigned by Hadrian.

Other restoration was done under Septimius Severus and by Caracalla in the 3rd century.

On March 16, 609 A.D., Pope Boniface IV, with the permission of the Emperor Phocas, changed the pagan temple into a Christian church, bringing the bones of many Christians from the catacombs and dedicating it to "St. Mary of the Martyrs," thus ensuring the preservation of the building to this day.

In 1929 the church, as a result of the Lateran Treaty, assumed the title of the Basilica Palatina, or more properly, the national church of all Italians.

17, 18 - Castel Sant'Angelo. What looks like an impregnable fortress was created by the Emperor Hadrian as his tomb. The Mole of Hadrian, or "Hadrianeum", was begun in 123 A.D. and held the remains of the Imperial family until Caracalla (217 A.D.) The story of the Mausoleum of Hadrian closely follows that of the city of Rome: the struggles and treachery of the Middle Ages, the splendor of the Papal Court and the Renaissance, the horrors of the Sack of Rome of 1527, the intense bombardment during many sieges, and the fireworks of many celebrations. The transformation into a castle probably occurred in the 10th century, when it became the possession of Alberic and his mother, Marozia, powerful figures in Rome at the time. It then passed to the Crescenzi family and in 1277 was occupied by Pope Nicholas III, who joined it to the Vatican by the famous passetto (passageway), a corridor which runs atop the wall that encircles the Vatican.

19 - The beautiful **Egyptian obelisk** erected on Quirinale Hill, across from the grand palazzo that is the office of the Presidency of the Republic, between two colossal Roman-era groups of horse break-ers, creates a powerful scene with the granite basin in front of it.

20 - The **Appian Way** is the Roman road which has the greatest number of interesting archaeological, artistic and natural fea-tures. Known as the "Regina Viarium", it was begun by Claudius in 312 BC.

21 - Aerial view of the **Isola Tiberina**, where the church of St. Bartholomew stands on the ruins of the celebrated Temple of Aesculapius, the Greek God of medicine, once a pilgrimage site for the diseased. Two bridges join the island to the rest of the city: Ponte Fabricius (also known as Quattro Capi), built in 62 B.C. and still intact today, and Ponte Cestio (46 B.C.).

22 - A picturesque **Roman sunset**, dominated by the char-acteristic silhouette of the domes. In the foreground, the cupola of the Church of San Carlo al Corso, and in the back-ground Michelangelo's cupola on Saint Peter's in the Vatican.

23 - **The Basilica di San Clemente** is among the most interesting churches in Rome from both an artistic and histori-cal point of view. The highlight of the basilica is the apse mosaic, which repre-sents, in a prodigious synthesis of pagan and Christian figurative elements, the scene of the Redemption, a masterpiece of the Roman school of the 12th century.

24 - **Santa Maria in Cosmedin**, one of the gems of medieval Rome, stands on the ruins of a Temple to Hercules, visible in the crypt of the church. The suggestive and austere interior is a good example of an early church (8th century). The elegant 12th century campanile (bell-tower) is in the Romanesque style. On the left side of the portico is a marble mask called the Bocca della Verità (Mouth of Truth).

25, 26, 27, 28, 29, 30, 31, 32 - The greatest church in Christendom, **St. Peter's Basilica**, rises on the gran-diose St. Peter's Square. Michelangelo's mighty sil-ver-blue *dome* dominates the scene, blending into the sky above, conveying a sense of the absolute and infinite, which touches the soul of all who gaze upon it. The construction of the dome proceeded through problems and obstacles of every kind. Michelangelo was already quite old when he began the proj-ect in 1546, and when he died in 1564 only the drum had been com-pleted.

The rest of the work was fin-ished between 1588 and 1589 by Giacomo della Porta and Domenico Fontana.

The *colonnade* is Bernini's most beautiful work, and forms the solemn entrance to St. Peter's and the Vatican.

The two great open semicircular wings seem as if they were the outstretched arms of the church, receiving all of mankind in one universal embrace.

If some of Bernini's other works appear to be extravagant, this colonnade shows the height of his genius.

He also designed the 140 statues of saints that decorate the colonnade, which were sculpted with the help of his pupils.

Pope Sixtus V (1585-1590) chose Domenico Fontana to oversee the erection of the *obelisk* in the middle of the piazza, a consid-erable task which aroused wonder and great enthusiasm in the people.

The obelisk measures more than 25 meters in height and was brought from the nearby ruins of the Circus of Nero.

The two fountains, the one on the right designed

by Maderno (1613) and the one on the left by Carlo Fontana (1675), harmonize beautifully with the vast square.

The Borghese Pope Paul V commissioned Maderno (1607-1614) to construct the broad *façade* of the church, and had his name and title written in very large letters across the entablature.

The *high altar*, under the cupola, rises above the Tomb of St. Peter, which was definitively identified after excavations in the 1950's.

In front of the tomb, ninety-nine lamps burn day and night; opposite is the crypt, designed by Maderno, rich with inlaid marble.

Above the altar rises Bernini's fantastic *baldacchino* (1633) (photo 27), supported by four spiral columns, made from bronze taken from the Pantheon.

But the glorification of the tomb of the humble fisherman from Galilee is the majestic dome that soars toward the heavens.

In the Tribune, four Doctors of the Church support the Throne of St. Peter, a stunning work in gilded bronze by Bernini.

The length of the interior of the basilica is 186.36 meters.

The vault is 44 meters high; the dome, measured from the inside, measures 119 meters, with the lantern adding another 17 meters; the perimeter of one of the four piers that support the dome measures 71 meters.

33 - St. Peter's Basilica. In the first chapel of the right nave is **Michelangelo's Pietà** (1498-1499). The deep pathos that animates the group, in which the eternally young Mother and the dead Son leaning down in her arms make an indissoluble whole, reminds us that this subjet was strongly felt by Michelangelo.

34 - The Sistine Chapel. The Last Judgement, commissioned by Pope Paul III, was begun by Michelangelo in 1535 and completed in 1541. Three hundred figures swarm in a composition which has an amazing coherence and clarity and in which space is organized into a real architectural structure of figures. Christ, the implacable judge, dominates this grandiose scene, his right arm raised in the act of condemnation.

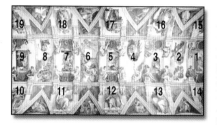

35 - The Ceiling of the Sistine Chapel:
1) Separation of Light from Darkness; 2) Creation of the Sun and the Moon; 3) Creation of Trees and Plants; 4) Creation of Adam; 5) Creation of Eva; 6) Original Sin; 7) Noah's Sacrifice; 8) Noah's Flood.; 9) Drunkenness of Noah; 10) Gioele; 11) Eritrean Sybil; 12) Ezechiele; 13) Persian Sybil; 14) Geremia; 15) Libyan Sybil; 16) Daniele; 17) Cuman Sybil; 18) Isaia; 19) Delphic Sybil.

36 - San Giovanni in Laterano, the Cathedral of Rome, was founded by Constantine as the Basilica of the Savior, during the papacy of St. Sylvester (314-335). It was destroyed and rebuilt several times; the current basilica dates to the 17th century. The imposing facade in travertine was built in 1735 by the architect Alessandro Galilei.

37 - San Giovanni in Laterano. The vastness of the central nave has as a background an imposing tabernacle (late 14th century), decorated by twelve small frescoes attributed to Barna da Siena. Above, the relics of the heads of Sts. Peter and Paul are kept in precious silver containers.

Under the tabernacle is the papal altar made under Pope Urban V in 1367.

38 - The Basilica di San Paolo. with its Vassalletto's **Cosmatesque Cloister** (restored in 1907), is among the most significant examples of Roman marble work: a genuine masterpiece for its fine molding and the richness and elegance of its carvings and mosaics.

39 - The inside of the Basilica di San Paolo, split into five naves, is opulent and impressive; the eye seems to lose itself in the unending line of columns, among which a mystic light flows from the double row of alabaster windows.

The Gothic Style canopy, which stands on four porphyry columns, is a 13th century masterpiece by Arnolfo di Cambio.

40 - The Basilica di Santa Maria Maggiore, the fourth largest church in Rome, is the only basilica which still retains its original shape and character. The beautiful façade of the Basilica, by Fuga, features a portico with five openings divided by pilasters decorated with columns, and a loggia with three great arches. The Romanesque campanile (bell-tower) is the tallest in Rome.

41- The church of San Pietro in Vincoli was built under the generosity of an Imperial matron, Eudoxia, daughter of Theodosius the Younger and wife of the Emperor Valentinian III. The chains used by Herod to hold Peter were sent to Eudoxia by her mother, who had received them from the bishop of Jerusalem. To house the chains, the young Eudoxia built the basilica. Inside the basilica is the tomb of Pope Julius II by Michelangelo. At the center is the statue of Moses.

42 - An aerial view of the Capitol. The square designed by Michelangelo was conceived as a vast terrace opening on the city. The Capital is reached up the flight of steps called the Cordonata (photo on the left) designed by Michelangelo and framed by ancient Roman statues.

44, 45, 46, 47 - Piazza Navona, or Circus Agonale, traces the shape of the Stadium of Domitian, which once occupied this site and held 30,000 spectators (photo 47). Three magnificent fountains decorate the piazza.

In the center is the Fountain of the Four Rivers by Bernini, who designed it as a base for the Egyptian obelisk which was brought here from the Circus of Maxentius. Four figures seated on the rocks represent the Nile, Ganges, Danube and the Rio de la Plata.

The fountain on the south side of the piazza, called the Fountain of the Moor (photo 44), was designed by Giacomo della Porta between 1571 and 1576, but his statues of tritons and masks were later moved to the Giardino del Lago in the Villa Borghese; the statues on the fountain are 19th century copies. The fountain takes its name from the statue of the Moor, which Bernini added in the 17th century.

At the north end of the piazza is the Fountain of the Calderari (Coppersmiths), so-called because of the many workshops in the area. This fountain also lost some of its original statues.

The church of Sant'Agnese in Agone (photo 45 and 46) is a magnificent example of the Baroque style by G. Rainaldi and Borromini. It was built on the site where, according to tradition, the virgin was stripped naked before being martyred, and miraculously hair grew to cover her body.

Underneath the church are remains of a primitive church and the Stadium of Domitian.

43 - Piazza del Campidoglio was designed by Michelangelo for the magnificent Pope Paul III (1534-1549). The old artist placed on a new pedestal the equestrian statue of the Emperor Marcus Aurelius (161-180), the only surviving example of the many bronze equestrian statues which once adorned Rome.

48, 49, 50 - The Trevi Fountain. Legend has it that a foreigner who tosses a coin into the fountain ensures his return to Rome. Set against a large building, the fountain is decorated with bas-reliefs and statues that stand upon mighty rocks from which the water

gushes. Spurts and roars animate the impressive scene.

It was Agrippa who brought the Acqua Vergine to Rome in the 1st century B.C., by way of an aqueduct.

The fountain was built by Nicola Salvi (1735) under Pope Clement XII, and was decorated by several followers of Bernini.

In the center, the Statue of Oceanus standing on a shell drawn by sea horses; in the lateral niches, Abundance (on the left), and Health (on the right), both by Filippo Della Valle.

51 - The Borghese Gallery. After the election of Paolo V Borghese as pope, his young nephew Scipione was made cardinal. Among the many titles which he held in that period, Scipione was entrusted with care of the art collection and cultural treasures of the pontifical court. With the help of two able architects, Flaminio Ponzio and Giovanni Van Santen (Vasanzio), Cardinal Scipione created the park and built the Casino Borghese, today the site of the Borghese Museum and Gallery.

52 - Museo Borghese. Two famous early works by Bernini (1598-1680).

Apollo and Daphne (on the right), finished by Bernini in 1622, perhaps marks the high point of his career. The Rape of Proserpina (on the left), which was inspired by Ovid.

53 - The Pauline Fountain was built for Pope Paul V by G. Fontana in 1611. The huge semicircular basin was added in 1690 by Carlo Fontana.

54, 55, 56 - Piazza di Spagna and the enchanting Spanish Steps. At the top of the steps is the church of the Trinità dei Monti, with its two cupolas (1495), and an Egyptian obelisk in front, brought here from the Sallustian Gardens in 1789. Inside the church is a fresco of the Deposition, a masterpiece by Daniele da Volterra.

The staircase built by Francesco de Santis, starting in 1723, is made up of 138 steps.

At the foot of the staircase of Trinità dei Monti, the "Spanish Steps", we find the Fontana della Barcaccia (photo 54). This is the work of Pietro Bernini, who created it around 1629, probably with the aid of his famous son Gian Lorenzo.

According to tradition, the unusual fountain shaped like a semi-submerged boat was ordered by Pope Urban VIII Barberini to commemorate a boat that had ended up stranded in the square during the great flood of 1598. In reality, the idea of depicting the boat as it is sinking was dictated by Bernini's genius, since he had to solve a technical problem: in fact, here the pressure of the Vergine aqueduct was rather low, and it was necessary to create a fountain beneath the ground level.

57 - The Fontana del Tritone at Piazza Barberini. An airy and felicitous synthesis of Baroque taste, the fountain is one of Gian Lorenzo Bernini's masterpieces, set in the center of the piazza opposite Palazzo Barberini in 1642. The triton that gives its name to the fountain is borne up by four dolphins as he blows into a shell to proclaim to the world the glory of the noble Bernini family.

58 - The superb Palazzo Farnese on the piazza of the same name, was begun during the papacy of Paul III by Antonio da Sangallo the Younger (1514), continued by Michelangelo (1546), who added the marvelous cornices, the central window and part of the courtyard, and then completed in 1589 by Giacomo della Porta.

59 - The immense Quirinal Palace was begun by Pope Gregory XII in 1574, and served as a residence to the popes until 1870, then to the king of Italy after the declaration of Rome as the nation's capital, and finally to the President of the Republic since 1946.

64 - One of the most famous streets in the world, Via Veneto is known for its elegance. Via Veneto, in front of Villa Borghese park, is a symbol of the "dolce vita" that characterized life in the capital during the 60s, when the stars of the sweet life such as Ava Gardner, Sofia Loren, Marcello Mastroianni, Anouk Aimée and Helmut Berger spent their evenings in its cafes and fashionable locales.

60 - Piazza del Popolo was designed by Valadier at the beginning of the 19th century.

At the center is the second Obelisk brought to Rome by Augustus, which was erected here by Fontana during the papacy of Sixtus V.

65 - Piazza della Repubblica. Initially called Piazza Esedra because of its shape which follows the curve of the exedra of the ancient Baths of Diocletian, was built at the time of the great renewal of Rome when it became the capital after the unification of Italy.

61 - The Palazzo Chigi and the Antonine Column or Column of Marcus Aurelius. The spiral frieze of the Column portrays Marcus Aurelius' campaigns against the Marcomanni, Quadi and Sarmatians.

Erected in his honor in 193 AD, the monument also recalls Antoninus Pius, the adoptive father of Marcus Aurelius who was emperor from 138 to 161 AD.

62 - Via Giulia. A long street built by Pope Julius II in the 16th century to replace the winding narrow streets that previously linked the Vatican to the Capitol.

The ivy-covered bridge of the Farnese, a broad arch that creates a romantic view of the street. It was created in 1603 to join Palazzo Farnese with other buildings across the street.

66, 67, 68 - Piazza Venezia, takes its name from Palazzo Venezia, built in 1455 by the Venetian Pope Paul II (1461-1471), while he was still a cardinal.

The Vittorio Emanuele II Monument (also called the "Vittoriano"), was designed by Giuseppe Sacconi (1885-1911). It rises from the foot of the Capitol Hill, where it was squeezed into the heart of the city, forever changing the relationship between this hill and its surroundings.

The Venetian sculptor Chiaradia worked for twenty years on the equestrian statue of the king, which was completed by Gallori (1901) after the death of the artist. The elaborate bas-reliefs on the base, which represent the most famous Italian cities, were designed by Maccagnani, who for many years collaborated with Sacconi in carving the three-dimensional ornamentation. The building's two colossal chariots are surmounted by winged Victories, whose dark bronze contrasts with the white marble and makes them visible against the Roman skyline. They were made by Carlo Fontana and Paolo Bartolini in 1908.

63 - Il Gianicolo, which offers some of the finest views of the city. Over the undulating sea of roofs, the numerous domes of Rome are silhouetted against the distant backdrop of the mountains, while the Tiber and its turns mark the city's unmistakable shape. On the great panoramic piazza is a monument to Giuseppe Garibaldi.

In the center is the Altar of the Fatherland, crowned by the statue of Rome, at whose feet since 1921 lies the Tomb of the Unknown Soldier.

69 - **Campo de' Fiori**, with its lively daily market is still a typical corner of old Rome today.

73 - The **lake in the EUR** with, in the background, the Palazzo dello Sport, built by M. Piacentini and P.L. Nervi for the Olympic Games in 1960.

70 - **Campo de' Fiori** is the site where the death penalty was carried out in Pontifical Rome. On February 17th, 1600, Dominican friar Giordano Bruno was burned at the stake here, accused of heresy by Pontifical Tribunal. The monument dedicated to the philosopher placed in the piazza's center is by Ferrari (1887).

74 - The **Palazzo della Civiltà e del Lavoro** in the EUR district, built between 1938 and 1943, is commonly called the "square Colosseum" for the 216 arches that characterize its four broad façades. The Castor and Pollux groups placed at the sides of the two stairways are another obvious reference to the architecture of Ancient Rome.

71 - A characteristic corner of **Trastevere**, where traditional handicrafts live on in apparent contrast with the modern metropolis.

75 - Evocative **Roman panorama** at sunset from the Pincio Terrace, which provides a magnificent view: in the distance can be seen the outlines of St. Peter's Basilica and the Vatican topped off by Michelangelo's cupola dominating the horizon.

72 - **Villa Borghese**. Shaded by the lofty trees in the most secret recess of the **Giardino del Lago**, a little classic-style temple is reflected in the green waters of an artificial lake.